Marriage Counseling Secrets

7 Heart Winning Secrets of Improving Communication with Your Spouse and Build a Long-lasting Relationship

By

GoldInk Books

BEFORE YOU START READING, DOWNLOAD YOUR FREE DIGITAL ASSETS!

Be sure to visit the URL below on your computer or mobile device to access the free digital asset files that are included with your purchase of this book.

These digital assets will complement the material in the book and are referenced throughout the text.

DOWNLOAD YOURS HERE:

www.GoldInkBooks.com

GOLDINK BOOKS

GoldInk Books is a self-publishing company. We produce books in a range of genres with efficiency, speed and convenience of digital publishing. Our researchers and authors are dedicated to bringing high-quality research to people all over the world. All of our books are available to read and download online. We use technology to make the book publishing sector more accountable. We are known for taking a serious and intellectual approach to different topics with popular appeal. To strengthen the pillars of knowledge, we want to put a book in everyone's hands and create an active network of digital creative communities.

© **Copyright 2021 by GoldInk Books - All rights reserved.**

This document is geared towards providing exact and reliable information in regard to the topic and issue covered. The publication is sold with the idea that the publisher is not required to render accounting, officially permitted, or otherwise, qualified services. If advice is necessary, legal or professional, a practiced individual in the profession should be ordered.

From a Declaration of Principles which was accepted and approved equally by a Committee of the American Bar Association and a Committee of Publishers and Associations.

In no way is it legal to reproduce, duplicate, or transmit any part of this document in either electronic means or in printed format. Recording of this publication is strictly prohibited and any storage of this document is not allowed unless with written permission from the publisher. All rights reserved. The information provided herein is stated to be truthful and consistent, in that any liability, in terms of inattention or otherwise, by any usage or abuse of any policies, processes, or directions contained within is the solitary and utter responsibility of the recipient reader.

Under no circumstances will any legal responsibility or blame be held against the publisher for any reparation, damages, or monetary loss due to the information herein, either directly or indirectly.

Respective authors own all copyrights not held by the publisher.

The information herein is offered for informational purposes solely and is universal as so. The presentation of the information is without contract or any type of guarantee assurance.

The trademarks that are used are without any consent, and the publication of the trademark is without permission or backing by the trademark owner. All trademarks and brands within this book are for clarifying purposes only and are owned by the owners themselves, not affiliated with this document.

Table of Content

INTRODUCTION 9

CHAPTER 1: IS IT WORTH THE EFFORT? 14

1.1 Why is Marriage Hard? 15

1.2 Perks of Marriage 17

CHAPTER 2: SAY YES TO ACTIVE COMMUNICATION 26

2.1 Active Listening 28

2.2 Active Speaking 32

2.3 Non-Verbal Cues 34

CHAPTER 3: SAY YES TO UNDERSTANDING 38

3.1 Look Inside Yourself 40

3.2 Learn Your Partner's Love Language 42

3.3 Nurture Curiosity in Yourself 44

3.4 Practice Empathy for Your Partner 46

3.5 Honestly Open Up to Your Partner 48

CHAPTER 4: SAY YES TO INTIMACY 51

4.1 Kinds of Intimacy 51

4.2 Make Moments Together 54

4.3 Learn to be Vulnerable 57

4.4 Show Physical Affection 60

4.5 Accept Your Partner and Avoid Comparison 62

CHAPTER 5: SAY YES TO MAKING TIME 65

5.1 Evaluate Quality Time 66

5.2 Share a Year Calendar 67

5.3 Put the Tech Away 68

5.4 Plan Date Nights Regularly 70

CHAPTER 6: SAY YES TO MANAGING FINANCES 73

6.1 Talk it Out with Your Partner 75

6.2 Combined or Separate Finances 77

6.3 Designate Fun Money 79

6.4 Create a Budget with Your Partner 79

6.5 Tackle Bills Effectively 83

CHAPTER 7: SAY YES TO APPRECIATION 85

7.1 Show Vocal Gratitude 89

7.2 Understand the Power of Small Gestures 92

7.3 Publically Acknowledge Your Partner 93

7.4 Keep a Gratitude Journal 96

CHAPTER 8: SAY YES TO FORGIVENESS 98

8.1 Set Your Perspective 101

8.2 Look at the Bright Side 102

8.3 Make Room for Empathy 105

8.4 Put Your Misery Behind Yourself 106

CHAPTER 9: WHAT TO DO AND WHAT NOT TO DO 108

9.1 The Don'ts of Marriage 108

9.2 The Dos of Marriage.. 113

CONCLUSION... **119**

Introduction

Did you know by any chance that 62 million people get married every year in the US alone? Did you also know every 13 seconds, there is a divorce in America?

What happened to all of the people who thought they were in love and wished to spend their whole life together? What went wrong?

I get to explore these questions every day while I sit with married couples trying to make their relationship work.

Being married, I understand that marriage comes with its complications, and it is not a ray of sunshine every day. Humans are imperfect and so are their relationships. Nevertheless, it does not mean that you and your marriage have to suffer. As a child, I was seriously affected by my parent's broken marriage. Their 20 year-long troubled marriage left me fighting with depression and anxiety. I had to go through many difficult years to come out of it. I remember on my career day in school when asked what I wanted to become. I said, I wanted to be someone who could make my mom and dad happy. Fast forward to today, I am a marriage and family counselor.

After healing myself from the trauma of bad parental marriage, I have been helping couples maintain a healthy marriage that gives them joy, excitement, and emotional intimacy. If you are having hiccups in your marriage, I understand what you feel. When you and your partner get home after a long day of work looking for some kind of reset and relief, you just cannot seem to achieve that in any way. Instead, the lack of connection and feeling of not being understood adds to the pile of exhaustion you bring from work.

Unsaid things become grudges and start to muddle with your thoughts. You do not feel seen. Sometimes you wonder if the person you once loved had turned into a stranger as you turn away from your partner in bed numbly. It is a mix of feeling too much and feeling nothing at the same time. You find yourself picking fights, and little things turn into days and weeks-long coldness. You then move to a friend to cry your worries away or search the internet to find you an instant revive to your marriage. You must have gotten you fair share of pieces of advice out of which some might have worked for your certain scenario and some just could not.

Finding the right advice is one thing but then trying to implement it in your relationship is another thing. Even the right advice, when not known how and when to execute, can bring you as much damage as the wrong advice.

These are the reasons I have written this book. I realized that I could reach only a limited number of couples through my job, but putting my knowledge and advice in a book can help me support more couples who are giving up on each other. For a marriage to be happy there cannot be just one tip that can magically make everything better. There is a great deal of effort and work that goes into a healthy marriage, but the fruits of it make it all worth it. I have put together seven secrets in this book that are fundamental for a fulfilling married life. You will get to know even if marriage is worth the effort, and if so, why? This part will help you understand what marriage can add to your life. Then I will break down the secrets of a satisfying married life, starting with active communication and understanding each other. After the cardinal steps of any relationship, we will move forward to emotional, intellectual, sexual, and experiential intimacy. Another great step is making time for your partner to relish experiences together and make each other more involved in each other's life.

It is about making new moments together in the framework of your daily life and outside of it. The fourth secret is managing your finances, with money being the number one cause of stress in a marriage. Moving on, appreciation goes a long way in a relationship. It is about making your partner feel wanted and cared for. It can spark the love you thought you had lost. The last secret is probably the most important one. It is forgiveness on the account that we are all human beings, and we cannot be perfect. It is the realization that sometimes the effort is enough. Lastly, we discuss the dos and don'ts in a marriage.

The first chapter of the book includes the perks of being in a marital relationship. The next seven chapters thoroughly discuss the importance of the seven secrets of a healthy marriage and how you can practice them in your life. The last chapter is dedicated to little tricks to keep your married life rewarding. My parents' marriage made me realize what a bad marriage can do to a couple and their kids, and my degree in marriage and family therapy gave me insight into the hidden reasons behind this unhealthy relationship and what are the ingredients that go into a healthy one.

I understand what kind of problems a marriage can pose because I have couples looking towards me every day to guide them and help them bring the spark back in their marriage. When I got married four years back, I got to implement the same secrets I have mentioned in this book to my marriage, and we both have never been happier. It is a beautiful experience to share your life with somebody and make heartfelt moments together.

My personal and professional knowledge has allowed me to write a book for you that can surely help you resolve your marital issues and allow you to feel understood and seen by your partner, nurturing a connection that you can cherish forever long.

Chapter 1: Is it Worth the Effort?

Everyone knows that even roses, arguably the most beautiful flowers on the earth, grow with thistles and occasionally end up in excrement. However, when it comes to friendships, we expect nothing less than absolute perfection from our companions. Impossible desires can be difficult terrain for developing relationships. The majority of couples who have been together for more than 30 years will confess that life is full of challenges. With challenges come tests that ensure and strengthen bonds.

Marriage is like a garden. It takes time to flourish, but those who carefully and lovingly tend to the soil get a rich harvest. It means that we need to put in the effort. You must make experiences together and work hard to write your life's tale together. What else will you talk about when you are old and sitting on your front porch sipping iced tea? The good and bad experiences both construct your vault of memories and lessons to pass down. There are no highs without lows.

Marriage comes with its complications. Here's why:

1.1 Why is Marriage Hard?

Everyone is looking for a magical potion to help them live a flawless life.

Having certain fantasies and thoughts as a child raises a person's expectations of life and their life partners. Marriageable age is usually between the second and third decades of life. This stage of young adulthood is marked by a surge of emotions that drive people to accomplish high heights in all aspects of life, resulting in a desire to be the greatest at everything. This also leads to a lack of patience and an aggressive approach to achieving goals. Understanding this component and being a little calculative will assist a person in balancing expectations through achievement.

Mental adjustment is another big factor. The mind adjusts to the body, and the body adjusts to the mind. For example, when you dine out at a restaurant, sometimes the body has to adjust to the extra oil and spices, but this can also sometimes cause discomfort or health problems. It demonstrates that the mind acknowledges the situation, and the body tries to adapt in order to conquer it. The way one thinks and what one desires is what tilts the adjustment balance. Inevitably, a person may begin to believe that their partner is not adapting, so why should they? Instead, if the thinking is slightly transformed in the face of difficulty to – "Let me consider and draw out a solution," the mind will seek solutions automatically. This will prevent the heart from going on a self-pity or sympathy trip, which can lead to complications.

Lastly, communication is a crucial component of a successful relationship. The male and female brains are clearly wired differently. This is determined by both hereditary and environmental factors. During counseling sessions, both spouses frequently remark that the other does not understand. Difference of opinion is unavoidable, but we have to deal with it in a healthy manner. Marriage, the most psychologically intense relationship most adults will ever have, is invariably a battleground for power and authority struggles. In a partnership where decisions regarding finances, childrearing, sex, and a variety of other topics must be made on a regular basis, conflicts are inevitable. In the everyday difficulties that plague married life, highly romanticized concepts of togetherness and bonding fade away.

But despite all the obstacles, if one manages to maintain a healthy marital relationship, how does his life look like?

1.2 Perks of Marriage

Marital responsibilities are viewed as extremely demanding in societies with high divorce rates. Before making a final decision, those who propose to marry, ponder long and hard. This is because they believe that marriage is a prison in which both the husband and the wife are confined to rigorous labor with no hope of release. They spend their time trying to find a way out through a crack in the wall and into the outside world. If you have the same views, let me try changing your mind:

- **Boosts Emotional Security**

    A loving and healthy relationship is built on the basis of emotional safety. It is all about building trust and feeling safe enough to be vulnerable and open with another individual.

    Simply expressed, emotional safety refers to a sense of security that allows you to fully express yourself with others and present yourself as your most genuine self.

    Emotional safety is a two-way street. When you feel emotionally safe enough to be yourself, it allows your partner to do the same. When both partners in a relationship feel secure, it creates a safe environment in which a deeper and more loving connection can develop. A happily married couple has a mutual sense of affection, trust, and protection. These are the factors that can help them build a strong foundation on which to develop their identities and achieve their life goals. Marriage also serves as a springboard for exploring and enjoying the previously unknown depths of human experience with the sense of security that only marriage can provide.

A husband quickly understands that he would be unable to traverse that perilous path into the future without the support of his female partner and companion, and it does the same for the wife. They feel ecstatic by believing that it will continue to be thus till the end of the journey. A secure marriage allows a couple to make plans for the next 20 or 30 years to attain their life goals. Because neither man nor woman is experiencing life's obstacles alone, a strong marriage helps to alleviate stress.

A person can do anything he or she wants as long as he or she is satisfied that his or her family and house are well protected and secure. Although they will have to give more time and attention to the challenges that come with married life, it will allow them to develop their bonds even further.

- **Boosts Happiness**

    A happy marriage is one of the life aspects that are most strongly and consistently linked to happiness. Because trustworthy companionship is a basic human need, good partnerships make people happy. Our happiness score will rise as our social interactions improve. In the study of positive psychology, there is widespread agreement that the number and quality of human interactions have the greatest impact on happiness. And it is in their marriage that a large majority of people find the greatest boost to their happiness.

    Over a 30-year span, the National Opinion Research Center in Chicago, Illinois, polled 35,000 Americans. Only 24% of single, divorced, separated, and widowed persons stated that they were "very happy" compared to 40% of married people. Of course, there is the factor that people who are already happy are more likely to marry and stay married. While this is possible, the researchers believe that it is safe to expect that marriage adds to happiness.

- **Boosts Mental Health**

    Married men and women are less likely to suffer from any type of mental disease. According to a 1991 mental health research in America, married people have much lower rates of severe depression and at least half the risk of getting any psychiatric condition than never being married, cohabiting, and divorced adults.

    Psychological stress and stress hormone levels are lower in married couples. In comparison to cohabiting and single women, married mothers feel more love and connection, have less ambivalence and have less conflict with their spouses. Moreover, people who are married are less prone to commit suicide.

- **Boosts Physical Health**

    Most of us consider eating a healthier diet and getting more exercise when we explore methods to improve our health. Few of us consider how to strengthen our bonds with our spouses or partners. However, a study reveals that the strength of our marriage can decide which of the two options we are more likely to experience when we commit to someone "in sickness and in health."

Brain Baker, a psychologist, has spent the last ten years researching the impact of marital stress on cardiovascular health. He followed both women and men with borderline high blood pressure for three years in one of his most recent research and discovered that blood pressure is strongly linked to what he terms "marital cohesiveness," or how much couples do and share together.

According to a previous study, couples in good marriages had thinner heart walls than those in failing marriages. A thicker heart wall leads to higher blood pressure.

According to a countrywide study of patients of all ages, married people are less likely to acquire heart disease than single, divorced, or widowed persons, regardless of age or gender. Even those who were married and had other risk factors, including high blood pressure, diabetes, smoking, or obesity, had a lower chance of heart disease. Researchers believe this is because people in happy, committed relationships have less stress and conflict in their daily lives.

Married people are more likely to detect symptoms, seek medical treatment, avoid dangerous behaviour, recover faster, and eat a healthier diet, according to researchers investigating marital health in seventeen different countries.

Moreover, emotional support is also beneficial to one's health. Researchers discovered that emotional support from a spouse could aid recovery from both small and serious illnesses, as well as aid in the management of chronic conditions.

The fact that spouses are intimately aware of and influenced by their spouse's choices is one of the major reasons marriages have such substantial health benefits. Couples, in a way, have a vested interest in looking out for one another and supporting healthy choices and behaviours.

- **Boosts Longevity**

    According to numerous studies, married people have a higher chance of living longer than their single counterparts. Marriage has been linked to a lower risk of death in research undertaken across a wide range of cultures. Almost every study of marital status and mortality finds that unmarried people of both sexes die at a higher rate, whether from accidents, self-inflicted wounds, or diseases, and this is true in every country that keeps accurate health statistics. The reasons why married people live longer are unknown. However, researchers theorized that the benefit could be due to the financial and health benefits of marriage.

- **Boosts Financial Status**

    Marriage is a significant step toward long-term financial stability. According to a study in the USA, marriage increases a man's earnings by 27 percent on average. Cohabiting families, split families, divorced families, and single-parent families all have lower incomes than married households. According to another USA study, married couples have a median household income that is twice that of divorced families and four times that of separated families.

- **Boost Emotional Intimacy**

    A strong emotional connection between spouses generates feelings of comfort, security, shelter, and mutual support. In times of stress, talking things out with a close, sympathetic partner may be very soothing. When you are feeling vulnerable, your attachment relationships might act as emotional barriers to stress and offer you stability.

Emotional connections make you feel appreciated and happy, which improves your mood. This mood enhancer has an impact on all elements of your life, from your mental health to how you treat others in your personal and professional life.

A boost in self-confidence is another advantage of an emotional connection between two loving couples. Your feeling of self-worth soars when you are comfortable and appreciated by your partner. Having someone you admire and respect, who recognizes your positive attributes enhances your self-esteem. This positive attitude not only affects your love life but also affects other elements of your life. People in loving, affirming relationships are more confident and capable of accomplishing personal and professional goals, according to research.

When you maintain a strong emotional bond with your partner, you develop an emotional support system as well. You will feel more capable and stronger in handling your life if you have someone to help you bear the emotional burden. This assistance increases your self-esteem, social abilities and makes you feel safe and secure in your life. In addition, research demonstrates that those in meaningful relationships with emotional support are less likely to experience stress and severe depression.

I hope that I have convinced you to some extent that marriage is worth a chance and it helps you secure a better and happier life. If you are having issues in your marriage and you want to develop a healthy and intimate connection with your partner, read through the next chapters.

Chapter 2: Say Yes to Active Communication

Although an ideal relationship does not exist, it has been discovered that through two certain factors, couples can develop a more pleasant relationship. Researchers examined over 2,000 individuals who were married, cohabiting, or in a long-term relationship in a recent study. 83 percent of the participants said they were satisfied in their partnerships and associated with the feeling of being equal partners in their union. Those same people said they were in a monogamous relationship with effective communication and healthy sex life, which they characterized as daily or weekly sex. We will discuss active communication now and sexual intimacy a bit later on. Let's get started.

Nobody is born with the ability to communicate naturally. Marriage communication, like cooking yourself a meal or driving a car, is a talent that can be learned. And the key to improving your relationship is good communication.

Communication in a relationship is like a river. It feels good and light when feelings and thoughts flow smoothly between marital partners. However, when communication flow is rough, it can be harmful and destructive. When communication is obstructed, pressure mounts.

Eventually, the thoughts begin to flow again, and then they tend to rush out in a destructive raging flood.

Couples often avoid uncomfortable conversations because they struggle with appropriate communication, especially when it comes to important issues. They exchange bits of information about who's going where and when and who's going to pick up the kids, but they never get into the talks that matter the most to them. The lack of a proper communication flow dries up their passion and affection with time. Couples in a great relationship chat freely, honestly, and feel comfortable sharing their most personal views. When issues occur, they comfortably and considerately express their concerns and feelings, and when things are going well, they express their positive views. Both parties speak in a courteous manner, avoiding aggressive, hurtful, or domineering remarks.

They pay attention and strive to understand what their spouse is saying with sympathy, rather than looking for flaws in what their partner is saying or ignoring what they hear, even if they disagree. After the conversation, both partners in the marriage feel good about it and that their problems have been heard and addressed. They even look forward to the chance to converse with one another, whether about minor matters or major concerns that will take a long time to resolve.

Moreover, you will see the good effects when you have a better "context" of each other and create a better understanding of each other. You will understand better what you both want in a relationship. When you discover a new "context," you can "select" to avoid the "potholes" rather than walking into meaningless arguments. Rather than doggedly walking into a pothole that both of you will later regret, you will prefer to understand the other person.

Now let's get into how you can have active communication with your partner.

2.1 Active Listening

Given how much listening we do; you would think that we must be experts at it! In fact, most of us are not, according to a study, we only remember about 25% to 50% of what we hear. That means that if you chat to your spouse for 10 minutes, they will only listen to around half of what you say.

When you turn it around, you will see that you do not hear the entire message either when you are given directions or given some other new information. You hope your 25-50 percent captures the critical details, but what if they do not?

Often, partners believe that they are terrific listeners. Many partners, however, are unable to provide an adequate account of what their partner said when asked. Partners are not always aware of their proclivity to plan what they will say next. If one partner is making a list of complaints or has been particularly unhappy, another partner is busy planning a defense. In this case, the failure to listen shifts the conversation's attention from the talking partner to the listener, and the dialogue becomes more about the listener's point of view rather than the partner's problem.

This often enrages the starter, and the conversation can quickly devolve into a back-and-forth, increasing dispute about who is right, as well as what the objective of the discussion is. Here are some strategies to keep in mind:

- **Ditch the Assumptions**

  When you are listening, try not to make any assumptions. Assuming entails coming to predetermined conclusions about the subject at hand. Before leaping to conclusions, double-check your understanding. Wrong assumptions can be like a train that has swerved off the track, and the conductor may be completely unaware of it.

- **Follow the Conversation**

    However, this appears to be a simple task, the majority of us fail to do so. We are so preoccupied with making our own case. "For example, if you are a Democrat listening to a Republican argue about government, your ears, like a debater, will be focused on what you disagree with. Debaters listen in order to demonstrate that they are correct and the other is incorrect. Couples should not follow the same suit.

    The sign that you have been debating maybe that you respond with a "Yes, but" or "I know, but."

    Listen to how you can agree. It is tempting to answer with arguments. You might have to force yourself to listen to what is right. Asking for further context can be helpful. According to a clinical psychologist who specializes in couple therapy, the listener must suppress their own emotional reactions and interpretations in order to truly grasp the essence of what the speaker is saying.

    Your partner may genuinely have a point you are not seeing because you are not listening thoroughly. Be prepared to admit that you may not have the complete picture.

- **Avoid Interrupting**

    We are often so preoccupied with our own thoughts that we cannot wait to speak up. Interrupting someone is a common mistake, especially when they have known each other for a long time. This diminishes the importance of their ideas and disregards their viewpoints.

- **Understand and Summarize What Your Partner Said and Felt**

    By summarizing what the other person said, you show that you are listening "what your spouse wants you to understand." Tell your companion what you agree with after paraphrasing, and then add your own opinions to the conversation with an "and" or "and at the same time." Now do the perception check. So, in addition to comprehending what your companion mentioned, make certain you comprehend how he feels. When your partner is just tired or frustrated, you may think he is angry with you.

- **Empathize**

    Pay attention with your heart. Empathy is defined as the recognition and understanding of a situation. "I can see how it would be frustrating/exciting/surprising to learn about," for example, demonstrates that you are paying attention to the emotions behind the words.

2.2 Active Speaking

Now that we know how you can listen to your partner effectively, we have to learn how to respond to your spouse in a meaningful issue-resolving manner. I have put together the following tips for effective speaking:

- **Pick a Good Time**

    It is all about the timing. Nevertheless, there is no such thing as the ideal moment to discuss, you do not want to bring up serious matters when your significant other returns home from work, is tired, or is watching television.

- **Validate Feelings**

    Instead of saying, "That was such a stupid thing you had to say the other night," use "I can understand why you were furious with me, and I want to talk about it with you."

- **One Issue at a Time**

    Avoid bringing up all of your problems at once. For example, the speaker can go from talking about her husband being late home to him not washing the dishes last week to him not doing something else at their wedding.

    Focusing on a single issue allows "your spouse to clearly respond to an issue and figure out how to change." Talking about all your problems at once, on the other hand, boxes your partner in, and they do not know where to go.

- **Use XYZ Statements**

    In situation Y, you do X, and I feel Z. The best remarks are those that are specific. So, when you tell your partner, "I feel really upset when we go to my mother's house and you do not say hello to my mother immediately away," he understands exactly how you feel, what the problem is, and what he can do.

- **Stick to "I" Statements**

    When a speaker uses the term "you," it causes the listener to become defensive and stop paying attention. Instead of stating, "You are so disrespectful to me," you can say, "I am uncomfortable with what happened last week."

- **Avoid "Never" and "Always"**

    Do not say anything like "You are always late" or "You never help out around the house" when you are talking.

2.3 Non-Verbal Cues

Body language is the conscious or unconscious communication of human feelings, emotions, attitudes, and thoughts through gestures, facial expressions, body movements, postures, walking styles, and distance.

It is an external manifestation of a person's emotional state. In a day, the average individual speaks for only 10 to 11 minutes, with an average phrase length of 2.5 seconds, but they can make and recognize about 250,000 facial expressions! When we communicate, the words we use account for 7%, tone of voice for 38%, and body language for a staggering 55%. You can keep the following non-verbal cues in mind to have a more engaging conversation with your partner:

- **Mirroring Body Language**

    When someone feels a bond with another person, their body language tends to match theirs. That is to say, if you are having a conversation with your significant other and they are making the same hand gestures and standing in the same posture as you, your conversation is probably going well.

- **Body Posture**

    A person's posture can unveil a lot about their mood. When your significant other leans in while you are talking, they are most likely to be interested in what you are saying. They are enthusiastically involved, and you typically have their undivided attention. They are more relaxed when they are reclined back while you are talking. They could still be engaged in the conversation, but their stance conveys a different tone.

- **Facial Expressions**

    When people are stressed, they sometimes clench their jaws and furrow their brows. There are a variety of reasons why someone comes to this point. It is possible that they do not like the direction in which the conversation is going. They might be anxious about the issue you are talking about. Alternatively, if you are not discussing anything that should be of concern to them, it could be a sign that they are not paying attention to what you are saying. It is also possible that they are preoccupied with something else that is making them stressed.

In addition, eye contact or the lack of it can reveal a lot about a person. When the other person makes eye contact with you as you speak, it usually means they are paying attention. It does not end there, though.

It is a prevalent idea that if someone is lying to you, they will not look you in the eyes. While this is sometimes accurate, the widespread belief has shifted the tide. Many people will do the exact opposite because you will not expect them to maintain eye contact while lying. They will make eye contact with you on purpose. This form of eye contact, on the other hand, feels forced, and the person frequently stares too long. It starts to feel uncomfortable. The final tip that I would like to give you is the 24-hour rule. The 24-hour rule is a simple and valid approach for preserving relationships, especially when acting on strong emotions.

We act on impulse from the limbic system in the brain, which is responsible for "fight, flight, or freeze." The idea is to slow down, breathe deeply, and activate the reasoning side of the brain. Instead of retaliating emotionally, give yourself 24 hours and speak things out calmly and rationally the next time you are "irritated" by or "mad" at your partner. You will keep your relationship intact while also improving your verbal communication skills.

Chapter 3: Say Yes to Understanding

Couples bond because they share a common idea of happiness. Couples stick together because they believe that they can make it work. Love, security, and trust are all qualities that people in partnerships crave.

As a couples' counselor, I believe there is a way to construct a fantastic relationship, but you cannot do it unless you fully understand your own and your partner's inner feelings. "Of course, I understand my wife," you would think to yourself, "she will make sure I remember everything I need to know about her." You may believe this to be understanding, but I call it avoiding information you do not want to hear. Understanding, on the other hand, is quite a different matter.

When partners complain to each other, it is because their needs are not being addressed. What are these needs? They differ from person to person. One spouse may feel unattached to her partner and desire to feel important to him. If her boyfriend was aware of this, he would most likely say something to make her feel better. It could be something like, "I am ecstatic to be with you." It does not take much to fill what is needed if you know what you are looking for. That is understanding. Unfortunately, when people are upset, it frequently sounds like this: "Hey, you did not pick up the dinner plates." Why do not you take out the trash on a regular basis?" These criticisms may provide insight into the feelings that lie beneath. She may feel ignored, depressed, and then angry, and all of these emotions manifest themselves in complaints about the dinner plates or the trash.

Most of us are not taught to analyse our internal feelings, particularly those that cause us to become irritated with our companions. Instead, we simply transform our unhappiness and disappointment into a complaint in the hopes of receiving something in return. However, the retaliation is frequently worse. No one likes being criticized. No one enjoys being judged. It is excruciating. In many relationships, we end up with hurt feelings on top of broken sentiments. When one person says something vexing, the other responds by ratcheting it up a notch. Both parties believe they have been duped and misunderstood. It is possible that this will become a pattern that couples will have to live with. They may justify, "It is not that horrible," but it is also not that good.

Some couples learn to deal with upset feelings by apologizing. It could be something like, "I am sorry I was harsh and said it to you," or something like that. This works to get the pair back on track until the next disagreement, but most couples do not know how to communicate what they want from their partner, so they end up frustrated.

Before the next argument begins, it may be helpful to learn what is going on inside the person. This is when the need for comprehension comes into play. She might be able to ask for it if she felt she needed to feel significant and valued by her partner. "Sometimes I feel like I am alone in this relationship, and it does not matter what I do," for example, "I understand, that is not the case, but could you please show me or tell me that I am important to you right now?"

Couples who can figure out what their partner wants, needs, or desires at the moment are more likely to provide it to him or her. Let's discuss a few ways you can incorporate into your life when it comes to understanding each other in marriage.

3.1 Look Inside Yourself

It is up to you to achieve whatever goals you have set for yourself in life. You have heard the expression, "You receive what you give." You cannot possibly understand another person if you cannot understand yourself.

In relationships, there is a constant give-and-take between each partner's demands for self-expression and intimacy. It is important to remember that we all want to be treated fairly.

Knowing what you want and how you want to be treated will help you treat your spouse appropriately.

Now, ask yourself, "What am I looking for?" How would I prefer to be treated? To me, what does justice involve? What irritates me the most? What makes me happy?

If you can understand yourself well enough to give appropriate answers to such questions, you can probably comprehend your partner as well. After all, we all want the same things: love, care, and happiness. Here are some tips that can guide you towards better self-understanding in a relationship:

- When you are having problems working out what you want in a relationship, think about what you do not want. That may not be as difficult as the first, making it easier to complete. Looking for what you do not like can sometimes work wonders.

- Relationships can be overwhelming at times. Because you love your partner, you find yourself doing things you would not ordinarily do. Consider whether you are happy doing it for him. You may not want to let up certain values because they help you grow.

- When you chat with other people, you usually get suggestions on how to act, what to do, or how to approach circumstances. It is easy for someone who has not been in your shoes to tell you how to work out what you want in a relationship logically. This is due to the fact that you may not be entirely focused on your own needs at the time.

3.2 Learn Your Partner's Love Language

Sometimes we feel as if we have put so much effort into our relationships that we have lost touch with our partners. Nothing seems to work, whether we show them love by expressing how we feel about them, doing extra chores around the house, or giving them a big hug at the end of a long day. Whatever you do to show your love for your partner, they simply do not reciprocate in the same way - why is that?

Dr. Chapman's popular relationship book "The Five Love Languages" emphasizes that we must communicate our love for one another in our spouse's "love language." This concept implies that everyone receives and understands love in their own language, and what makes us feel love is not always the same as what makes our partner feel love.

We may better understand our partner by discovering how they show us love and how we should show them love by better understanding the languages, thereby increasing the bond and communication in the relationship. Let's go over the five love languages if you do not know what they are. It will be easier to understand your partner's love language by doing so:

- **Words of Affirmation**

    This love language is straightforward: it involves using your words to communicate your feelings for someone. While you may believe that someone understands how you feel, someone who has this love language needs to be told how you feel - that you love them, that they are important to you, and that you enjoy who they are.

- **Quality Time**

    While this love language may appear to suggest spending more time with your lover, what it actually says is that the time you spend together is of high quality. It is time to put your phone down and look your partner in the eyes. It is time you said you would be there, and you are there. Quality time is the time that makes a person feel cherished, no matter how limited it is for someone whose love language is quality time.

- **Helping Out**

    To someone whose love language is acts of service, the words "Let me do that for you" or "Can I assist you with that?" are amazing. Anything you can do to make your loved one's life easier will make them feel loved.

- **Physical Touch**

    Physical touch love language may appear to be simple, yet there are layers to it. Yes, physical touch in partnerships frequently implies sex, but in this situation, touch can refer to a pat on the back, hug, or caressing someone's arm. Touch can be exciting, but it can also convey that you care and love someone.

- **Presents**

    If receiving presents is your partner's love language, they believe the giver of gifts is using the gifts to express how they feel. They believe that the thoughtfulness of the present and the time spent preparing it demonstrates how much their individual cares about them.

3.3 Nurture Curiosity in Yourself

Let's face it: your companion is special to you. You would not have chosen to be with them otherwise. You were probably drawn to them because of qualities that piqued your interest. Being intimate with someone entails maintaining an ongoing interest in who they are and how they think.

Curiosity and interest of this nature can also be employed during communication. You can spend some time connecting with your partner and critically exploring their choices, as well as allowing them to explore your thought process.

Listen to your partner as though he or she is telling you a story about someone else (even if it is about you). Become interested in how they are feeling, why they think the way they do, and how this affects them. Instead of focusing on how you might be feeling about what they are saying, try to concentrate your attention on them and their story.

Ask powerful, intriguing questions to elicit additional information from your partner about their thoughts, feelings, and experiences so you can have a better knowledge of them. Refrain from reacting or fighting back. If you are thinking about what you are going to say next, you are not listening to understand. We tend to become defensive and judgmental of what our spouse is sharing with us when we disagree or feel attacked. This can cause a conflict, misinterpretation of our partner, and eventually, a challenge to our relationship and intimacy.

We do not jump to assumptions as often in understanding relationships, and instead of being defensive, we might become intrigued about what our partner is sharing.

3.4 Practice Empathy for Your Partner

Empathy allows you to comprehend what the other person is going through. It allows us to put ourselves in someone else's shoes and imagine how or why they are feeling a certain way without having to experience the emotion ourselves. For instance, if your partner claims that something you said made them feel judged, but you did not mean to, empathy can help you understand where they are coming from, even if you disagree.

Listening to each other's feelings and thoughts on a frequent basis helps you establish empathy in a relationship. Seeing the world through your partner's eyes can help you develop a stronger bond and appreciation for their personality. Spend some time with your partner practicing this simple exercise to get started brewing this healthy relationship secret sauce. Write your answers to the following questions on separate sheets of paper. Wait till the end to help each other or share your responses.

- What makes your significant other happy? When they are joyful, how do they act? Are there any words or gestures that they utilize to express their feelings?

- What irritates your partner? How do people express their rage, or how can you tell if they are angry even if they do not?

- What are some of your partner's favorite pastimes? Are they competent in their field? Is it necessary for them to excel, or are they fine with merely doing it?

- What do you think your partner admires about you? What do you believe irritates them the most?

- What do you believe you could say or do to improve the quality of life for your partner?

Take some time to share your responses when you have written them down. Check to see if you came close to getting it perfect. Even if your answers were completely off the mark, you could still develop empathy in a relationship that is currently lacking in it. Listening—really listening—to your spouse when they talk is what you need to do to develop empathy. You can recognize that your partner has a right to their feelings, even if you do not agree with their beliefs or feel the same way.

3.5 Honestly Open Up to Your Partner

It is a lot easier to express your thoughts on intellectual information than it is to share your personal feelings and emotions. Both men and women have difficulty expressing their emotions, but male partners appear to have an even more difficult time with heart-to-heart communication.

It requires emotional risk and fortitude to share the depths of your heartfelt feelings, as it might make you feel vulnerable and exposed. However, expressing your sentiments is the very thing that will bond your relationship better. You can create deeper intimacy with your partner by communicating what is on your mind. You can follow the below tips to effectively communicate your views and thoughts with your partner:

- **Fear of Rejection:** If you are honest and open, you must let go of the possibility of rejection. Being vulnerable means being open, and you cannot be afraid of the outcome if you want to have an honest and open relationship. If you cannot be honest with the person you love because you are scared of what they might say or think, then the relationship is not right for you.

- **Use Statements Not Questions:** When it comes to your emotions, do not try to be evasive. As a passive-aggressive approach to getting the answer they desire, people may ask questions instead of making assertions. Instead, simply be honest with yourself by stating your desires in an "I" statement rather than a "you" statement. This will assist in clarifying any misunderstandings and allow you and your partner to get right to the topic.

- **Be Honest:** When it comes to crucial topics, be honest with your sentiments and do not lie to make them feel better. You are creating more issues than you are solving.

- **Feelings and Behavior:** Align your emotions with your actions. Consider how you are feeling on the inside. When you become emotionally educated with yourself, you may figure out how to link your feelings inside to your behavior outside.

- **No Confusion:** Do not be frightened to speak your mind. It is an important approach for you and your significant other to grasp what is going on and how it affects you. There should be no opportunity for misunderstanding when you communicate what you want, whether it has to do with the relationship or anything external.

These were the five strategies you can use to get to know your partner better and build a connection with them so you can support and love each other better.

Chapter 4: Say Yes to Intimacy

When you are in an intimate relationship with your spouse, you feel like you are at home with the other person. Only a few people in your life can have an intimate relationship with you because it entails exposing your sensitive side. It is about being your true self and loving each other unreservedly in an intimate relationship. You have probably heard the term intimacy used in relation to sex and romance. However, intimacy is not the same as sex. It is possible to have one without the other: intimacy without sex and sex without intimacy. There are various kinds of intimacy, including sexual intimacy. Let's get into them:

4.1 Kinds of Intimacy

- **Emotional Intimacy**

    Understanding, accepting, and loving your companion for who they are is emotional intimacy. You will feel comfortable and safe opening out to your partner if you are aware of their affection for you. Sharing your desires, feelings, and ambitions with your spouse will help you both get to know each other better and boost your chances of a long-term connection. It may take some time to form an emotional bond with your partner, but if you do not overthink it, it can be pretty simple. Consider spending time with your companion by discussing your hopes and dreams. Instead of being accusatory or judgmental, emotional closeness necessitates being open and honest with one another.

- **Intellectual Intimacy**

    Intellectual intimacy enables you and your partner to agree on significant life decisions and raise children who share your beliefs. This could imply that you and your children agree on healthy lifestyle choices, curfews, and so on. This level of closeness allows you to share information and learn a few traits from one another. It will help you both grow as individuals and as a team. You both have complete faith in each other's intelligence and would never consider undermining it. This type of intimacy can be developed through in-depth chatting about discussions about issues of mutual interest. It might be conversations about critical responses to themes such as books, politics, society, and what is going on around the globe. To improve intellectual connection, you might acknowledge your partner's comments and ideas in return. Talking about these difficult things might help you and your partner create mutual respect.

- **Recreational Intimacy**

    Recreational intimacy is when you and your partner do things you both enjoy. It might be that the two of you have a special place, that you enjoy sports, that you want to go to new areas, or that you prefer to go for a walk on the beach. Take up a hobby together, play sports together, or go on a vacation together to establish this intimacy. Even if the two of you want to join a gym or go on a trek together to help each other keep in shape, your physical and emotional health will improve, and you and your partner will have a great time together.

- **Physical Intimacy**

    Physical intimacy differs from sexual intimacy. It is basically showing affection for one another, which can range from holding hands to hugging to cuddling on the couch to kissing. Touch can help you relax by lowering cortisol levels.

    Physical intimacy may come first, followed by emotional intimacy, or vice versa. Some people believe they need to be physically intimate with their partner before they can open up with them, while others believe they need to be emotionally connected before they can do anything physical. Couples should start taking things slowly, such as hand-holding, kissing, or snuggling, to discover whether there is any romantic chemistry between them.

Intimacy is the most important element that the two of you can have if you want to have a long-term relationship. To both of you, intimacy can mean anything as long as it brings you closer than anyone else you know. It is as if you are living with a stranger if you do not have intimacy. Intimate relationships necessitate a significant amount of effort, time, and dedication. So, let's learn how you can achieve it.

4.2 Make Moments Together

Intimacy is not just about a physical relationship, as I mentioned previously. It is also about connection and familiarity. With that in mind, one of the finest ways to strengthen your relationship with your spouse is to enjoy new experiences together. You could, for example, collaborate on a large project like restoring or flipping a home. You might consider adopting a dog as a new member of your family. If you are not ready to make such commitments, consider taking a trip to a new country and exploring its depths together.

These experiences are meant to test you — they will drive you and your partner to work closely together, sometimes arguing or finding each other annoying along the way, all while strengthening your bond and boosting intimacy in your marriage. I have put together some more ideas you can try with your partner to develop a meaningful bond:

- **Cooking Together**

    Is not there an old saying that "The couple that cooks together stays together"? So, get your measuring cups and cookbooks ready to add some spice to your kitchen. If you and your spouse have children, try not to have dinner until the kids have slept at least once a month.

    Then, together, prepare your food and have a romantic dinner for just the two of you. Joining a cooking class together is a wonderful way to learn new recipes and cooking skills if you can get out of the house.

- **Exercising Together**

    There are numerous advantages to working out with others. You will not only be able to spend more time together, but you will also be able to improve your health, get in better condition, and even improve your sexual life.

After all, women have been linked to enhanced body image, short- and long-term arousal, and reduced sexual and erectile dysfunction through exercise.

This may be going for a walk together, exercising at home with an app, attending a yoga class, or enjoying a fitness game on a video game console.

- **Read Together**

Read a book together while curled up on the couch or in bed. Read aloud or quietly with a partner. For the two of you, have your own private book club. Over coffee or your favorite meal, chat about the books you are reading.

- **Renew Memories**

You have spent a long time together and will continue to do so in the future. Put aside some time to think about your lives as a couple. Take a look at your first images together by scrolling through your Facebook photos, phone camera, or Instagram photos.

Reminisce about all of the activities you have done and places you have been as a couple throughout the years, and keep scrolling until you reach your most recent images together.

4.3 Learn to be Vulnerable

Being able to connect with each other is one of the most rewarding aspects of being human. We are programmed to do it. We live in families, work in teams, fall in love in pairs, and thrive in friendships. Either we realize it or not, we all have a desire to connect. Despite this, we are witnessing an increase in loneliness, sadness, broken relationships, and alienation. What is going on?

Vulnerability is the power that propels connection. It is courageous. It is beautiful. Instead, we have turned it into a flaw.

Brene Brown is a research professor with a Ph.D. in psychology. She studied those who have a strong sense of belonging and connection, as well as those who do not. The difference between the two sets of couples, according to her research, was that individuals who felt a deep sense of belonging and love believed they were deserving of it. People who believed they were deserving of connection felt more attached.

People are more likely to approach others when they sense they are deserving of a relationship. They will be the first to express their love. They will say, "I miss you," right away when the relationship grows apart. They will want assistance and be receptive to others' love, affection, and influence. This is not to say that they will always get their way. Because they are less likely to feel ashamed, they are more willing to be vulnerable and open in relationships. People who believe they are deserving of connection are less likely to blame themselves and their own "worthiness" for the disconnection if the relationship falls short – if the "I love you" is left hanging, the "I miss you" is not returned, or the request for help is turned down. Here's how you can practice vulnerability in a relationship:

- Pay attention to what you actually desire and take steps toward it. It is the voice that comes from intuition, experience, and unspoken words. It is the bravest thing to go after what you want and be vulnerable to the risk.

- Ask yourself some questions. What would you do or say if you were not scared of being judged? What if you followed your heart? Tell someone you care about them. Telling someone you miss them is a good idea. Do you want more for yourself? How can you get rid of a hurtful relationship? How can you fight harder for your relationship?

- Examine your beliefs. Sometimes we believe things for such a long period that they become entrenched in our minds and refuse to leave. Check to see if they are still working for you. What might happen if you let yourself be vulnerable, open yourself, and take a chance? Too often, behavior is motivated by a desire to avoid shame - the desire to avoid getting any evidence that you are unworthy of love, connection, or receiving what you have requested. The more you believe you are undeserving, the more you will act as if it is real, and the more disconnected you will become.

4.4 Show Physical Affection

According to a 2017 survey, most American adults have sex once a week. This may not seem common, especially given how physical closeness is portrayed in entertainment. Sex is frequently depicted in movies and television as a simple experience that is easily sparked and executed. In truth, it is far trickier than that, as various factors are at play, including a couple's dynamics, physical chemistry, emotional connection, and so on. The truth is that judging what constitutes a healthy physical connection is entirely subjective to the persons involved. And sometimes, it takes some effort to improve physical intimacy. It is a process that necessitates a combination of energy, communication, and desire, which can be tough to summon in the midst of life's everyday stresses. You may kindle passion and deepen your relationship, no matter how many years pass, by having candid dialogues and exploring new sexual intimate experiences. Here are a few tips for you around the subject:

- Having an open and honest conversation with your spouse is one of the first stages toward physical intimacy. As it turns out, this conversation can help to clear up any misunderstandings that may be causing long-term damage to your relationship.

- When a partner displays mocking, disgust, mistrust, anxiety, or prejudice over tough or embarrassing mistakes, most people will begin to withhold intimacy over time. Both partners should know that they can always go to each other in a relationship, knowing that their flaws will be accepted without judgment.

- As you may recall from your early days of the relationship, sexual intimacy thrives on novelty and learning new things about each other. So, try to break up your routines and do new activities with each other so you may view each other in a fresh light and learn new things about each other.

- When you are in a committed relationship, especially one that you intend to keep for the long haul, sex is not only about having fun; it is also about maintaining a romantic bond. Try romancing each other as though you have only recently met. It is astonishing how much you can learn about each other if you start asking and listening more instead of assuming.

4.5 Accept Your Partner and Avoid Comparison

Even in healthy partnerships, 70 percent of problems are recurring and never resolved. Characteristics that one spouse has (or lacks) that irritate the other are frequently at the basis of these schisms. It is typically more effective to become more accepting of your partner's qualities and faults rather than trying to get them to change fundamentally when it comes to improving your relationship experience. Here are some pointers on how to become more accepting.

- Sometimes people can become irritated by traits or behavior of their partner that are not even that big a deal. It is easy to lose sight of that when frustration mounts.

- What are some of the annoying characteristics that your partner puts up with? It is easy to see everything through your own eyes in a relationship. You may see all the ways your partner irritates you, but you casually overlook all the minor ways you are a nuisance to live with.

- When one of your partner's flaws irritates you, it is usually because you are reading too much into it.

- Examine the extra meanings you are attaching to your dissatisfaction with your partner's imperfections. If you have an anxiety disorder, their shortcomings may trigger worry in you. If you are prone to feeling uncared for (due to earlier experiences), their shortcomings may exacerbate such feelings.

- What options do you have if your partner is not going to change fundamentally? Accepting your partner's imperfections can help you mentally move on to considering the practical alternatives. What can you do to decrease the influence of their shortcomings and weaknesses on you? What are the viable alternatives? How can you decrease your tension if your partner is still going to show the same flaw?

There is a huge factor that we cannot overlook when it comes to accepting your partner and marriage. It is comparison. Try these strategies to stop the romantic comparison marathon to safeguard your intellect and emotions from destructive judgments:

- No relationship is perfect. We are constantly bombarded with images and talks of couples on romantic dates, kissing at sunset, or lavishly showering each other with gifts to commemorate an anniversary, but it is important to remember that these are just the highlights. Although it is uncommon for someone to post or talk about a fight with their partner, a boring Saturday night, or the fact that their anniversary meal caused them food poisoning, these things do happen.

- We have a tendency to view other people's triumphs through the lens of our own flaws, which is something we are not always conscious of but can be extremely harmful. This implies that we will compare our innermost insecurities to what we consider as the best about someone else, and sometimes we tend to project these insecurities on our partner.

- Always be truthful to yourself about your needs and wants. We frequently make comparisons because we are interested in what other people think or because we see something we want even though we might not have known we wanted it before seeing it. Take a step back. Reconsider your choices. Be mindful that no two people are alike and that no two relationships are alike.

I hope these tips and strategies helped you get a better perspective on the concept of intimacy and how to nourish it.

Chapter 5: Say Yes to Making Time

When you first get married, your mind is filled with all the wonderful things you will be able to accomplish as a couple now that you have finally arrived at the long-awaited state of "spending our whole lives together."

Despite our best efforts, the dream does not always match reality in marriage. Perhaps more often than not, it entails stolen moments together after work or rushed periods in between juggling meals, grocery shopping, and childcare. When we do get that valuable time together, most of our talk and activities can be focused on practicalities, plans, or household duties. Quality time spent together is often in scarcity.

Researchers from the University of Minnesota researched 47,000 couples from 2003 to 2010, according to a recent publication in the Journal of Marriage and Family. What did they discover? When couples spent time together, they were twice as happy in their lives. The study revealed that when both partners spent time together, their stress levels dropped dramatically, and they perceived their lives to be more meaningful.

Lacking time for your partner appears to be a sign of trouble, according to research. Time is one of three challenging issues for couples in their first five years of marriage, according to a study (the others are sex and money.)

Do you believe that your marriage requires you two to spend more time together? Then the following strategies will help you.

5.1 Evaluate Quality Time

If you wish your relationship to be healthy, you must learn to recognize the signs that you and your partner need to spend more quality time together. The following are some of those signs:

- You are constantly on your phones.
- You place a higher priority on friendships or activities than spending quality time with your spouse.
- At significant events, you are not together.
- You are arguing more or do not feel connected.
- You do not plan date nights or make plans.
- You are unhappy.

If your marriage has any of the above signs, realize that spending quality time together can help to counteract the bad consequences.

5.2 Share a Year Calendar

Draw up a family calendar at the end of each year, preferably in the final week of December, in which you add the projected number of minutes you will strive to spend with each other every week, followed by the actual number of minutes you will spend with each other in a week.

Make a promise to each other to do your best and stick to the schedule. This will enhance the likelihood that you will take the whole thing seriously. Each of you should keep a copy of the calendar in a prominent location where you will see it every morning. Remind your partner of his or her commitment when you get up in the morning and vice versa.

Be mindful of how much quality time you spend together and write it down on the calendar. Evaluate at the end of every month to see if you are on track to reach your goals. It will warn you that you need to back up if the number of minutes you spend with your spouse is significantly less than the number of minutes you wanted to spend with him or her. A week has 10,080 minutes. Your goal should be to spend 1,000 to 2,000 minutes a week together.

5.3 Put the Tech Away

It is a simple concept that is more complex than it appears. We rely largely on rapid pleasure as a society. We strive to know what is going on in the world right now, what our friends and family are up to when our packages are being delivered, how many steps we walk in a day, and so on, but we do not pay attention to what or who is right in front of us. Put your phones on the table.

Social media is not going away, and your newsfeed will be there for you to check later on. The advantage of having little computers at our disposal is that we can access information at any moment. Our own anxiousness makes us feel compelled to need to know everything "right now." Spending time with your partner should be enjoyable for both of you. How do you go about doing that?

When you put your phone away and come to a complete stop, something extraordinary happens: you become fully immersed in the present moment. As a result, being aware of the present and appreciating the "now" because phones, laptops, tablets, and other electronic devices distract us from one another, this is especially crucial in partnerships.

We often make excuses like, "Oh, I will tell them later," but later rarely comes, and things are frequently left unsaid, leading to hidden animosity.

One of the most basic factors of a healthy relationship is communication. Your urge to have your phones on you 24 hours a day, seven days a week is impeding your willingness and capacity to spend time with your spouse.

Picking a time when you and your partner are most available is one of the simplest ways to start adopting this principle. It could be late at night after work or early in the morning before work. Set aside time each day to talk with each other in a safe environment, and establish a secure location to store your phones during this time. Inquire about their day, discuss their previous week, and discuss the weather. Talk about anything you want. You are providing each other undisturbed time, attention, and focus by doing so. All of this appears to be basic and straightforward, but it is quite effective. Some of you might think to yourself, "Who has time for this?" when you read this. This does not have to be a one-hour affair. Begin with 10-15 minutes. After that, aim to gradually increase your time as the days pass. You may be able to devote more time to this on some days than others.

The notion is more important than the timeline. The more you value communication with one another, the more it will become normal and ordinary in your daily life.

Making time for your spouse will also not seem like a chore in this way.

5.4 Plan Date Nights Regularly

When partners spend time together, they have a stronger sense of contentment and less stress. Include a date night in your weekly schedule as one of the most important relationship tips for a successful relationship.

According to the National Marriage Project, having a weekly date night might help your relationship look more exciting and minimize boredom. It also reduces your chances of getting divorced, improves your sex life, and promotes healthy communication. The following are some excellent date night suggestions:

- Recreate your first date if you have not already. Return to the same restaurant and order the same dish as when you first met. Pretend you are strangers meeting for the first time to spice up your evening.

- When you stroll down memory lane, you bring up a rush of recollections and feelings; both expressed and unexpressed. There is a good possibility you have forgotten about the chemistry you two shared on your first date. You will undoubtedly have some laughter, emotional moments, and exciting experiences with one another.

- Plan a weekend getaway. While traveling the world together is a romantic ambition, you might start with spending a vacation in a nearby hamlet or town. Take a trip to the beach. For the time being, put technology aside and enjoy the sun, the greenery, and your partner by your side. Traveling together will allow you to make even more amazing memories. It will also help you realize that there is more to life and that you and your partner need to get out and enjoy it. There is nothing like traveling with your significant other.
- Make it your mission to try and rate all of the Mexican eateries and Italian trattorias in your area.

Moreover, one of the most constructive strategies to stay close and connected is to focus on something you and your spouse care about outside of the relationship. Volunteering for a project, cause, or community service that both of you value can help to keep a relationship fresh and exciting. It can also introduce you to exciting new people and ideas, allow you to collaborate on new challenges, and provide you with new ways to communicate with one another. Doing things to help others gives you a lot of pleasure while also easing tension, anxiety, and despair. Humans are hardwired to help others. The more you help, both individually and as a couple, the happier you will be. So, use whatever strategy works for you to spend more time together. Think about your life without your partner. This will help you put down your phone and skip time-wasting meaningless activities.

Chapter 6: Say Yes to Managing Finances

According to Kansas State University studies, arguing about money is "by far" the most important predictor of whether you stay as a couple or not. According to studies, those arguments take longer to recover from and are more intense. With two paychecks and two financial situations colliding, managing money as a couple may be difficult. Here's a list of the most frequent financial challenges that married couples face to pave way to healthier marital economics and relationships:

- When both spouses work and cannot agree on financial matters or find the time to discuss them, they may decide to split the expenses or assign them in some other fair and equitable manner. After the debts have been paid, each spouse is free to spend the remaining funds as they see fit. Although, it appears to be a logical idea, the procedure sometimes breeds animosity toward the particular purchases made. It also divides spending power, removing most of the financial benefit of marriage, as well as the opportunity to plan for long-term goals like homeownership or retirement. It can also lead to destructive behaviors such as financial infidelity, in which one spouse hides money from the other.

Bill splitting also pushes off any planning and agreement-making about how financial responsibilities will be shared if one spouse decides to cut back on hours; loses a job; takes a pay cut to try out a new career; return to school, leaves the workforce to raise children, or care for a parent; or if there is any other circumstance in which one partner may have to financially support the other. You need to have a discussion about such scenarios far in advance of any of them occurring.

- Personality can have a huge effect on how people talk about money and how they spend it. Even if both partners are debt-free, the battle between savers and spenders can manifest itself in a variety of ways. It is critical to understand your and your partner's financial personalities, as well as to freely discuss any disparities.

- Most people arrive at the altar with financial baggage ranging from student loans to vehicle loans to credit cards to gambling habits. When discussing income, expenditure, and debt repayment, if one couple has more debt than the other — or if one partner is debt-free — conflicts can arise.

- Lastly, of course, there are major decisions revolving around the lifestyle and education of children, if you have any.

If you are having any issues while managing your finances, read through the following list.

6.1 Talk it Out with Your Partner

A successful marriage relies on effective communication. According to studies, couples who speak positively with each other have more marital happiness and less negativity in their relationship. If partners want to work together to address financial challenges, they must learn how to communicate successfully.

Listening to your partner without interrupting or distracting them is an important aspect of good communication. They should feel that you are completely focused on them. You must affirm your spouse's feelings, be honest, and be nice and courteous throughout conflicts if you wish to communicate effectively. Being approachable in this way will make your partner feel more at ease approaching you with financial concerns. So, what do you need to talk about with your partner? The following points:

- You might wish to go on a once-in-a-lifetime trip, put money into your family, or retire early. Whatever your aims are, work together to develop some common goals and clearly define what you both want to accomplish in the long run. Sitting down and drafting a money wish list is a terrific exercise to undertake together, whether you are newly married or updating your family's financial strategy.

- It is a good idea to keep track of all your joint expenses, such as water, electricity, and gas bills, as well as rental payments, as a married couple. Dinners out together or upcoming vacations are examples of this. Most of us, however, have personal expenses such as new clothes or nights out with friends that may not be covered by the marriage budget. Identifying which expenses are shared costs will help you avoid complications down the road.

- The truth is that we all have a money personality, as strange as it may sound. Some of us are born savers, while others are reckless spenders. Neither is inherently superior to the other. However, knowing your money personality is crucial since it will help you understand your spending tendencies.

- Understanding your and your partner's money personality will only help you avoid potentially dangerous activities like accumulating a large amount of debt. Big spenders, shoppers, savers, debtors, and investors are just a few examples of money personalities. It will help you figure out the best method to saving, investing, and developing a sound financial plan if you know which bucket you fit into.

6.2 Combined or Separate Finances

You can choose out of the two according to your preferences:

- **Combing Your Finances**

    In this situation, both of your incomes are placed into a joint checking account, and both of you are using the account and sticking to a budget that you have agreed upon. All of the money flows into and comes out of the same pot. To make this work, you and your partner must sit down, total your joint income, and then draw out and agree on a budget that covers all shared expenses, from groceries and bills to housing. You have complete financial transparency in this case.

This implies that you must also agree on discretionary expenditures. Because your finances are so connected, you need to accept and agree on your spending. You are on the same team, achieving the same objectives.

It does not matter whether one individual earns twice as much as their partner in this situation because the budget is balanced by your combined income. If one person's income increases while the other's decreases, the two will balance each other out. Because all cash and costs are deposited and taken from the same account, there is no difference between what is yours and what is mine.

- **Keeping Your Finances Separate**

    In this situation, your money does not mix with your partner's. You keep your bank accounts, budgeting, and bills separate. Both of you are in charge of your own finances. You do not have to rely on your significant other financially, and they do not rely on you. It will not affect your finances if your partner is not good at budgeting.

6.3 Designate Fun Money

Paychecks of both of you are deposited into a single account using this approach. All savings and payments are made from that account, but both of you have your own checking account where you receive monthly fun money.

You receive the advantages of integrating your funds (full transparency), but you have the freedom to buy whatever you want with your fun money. It is critical to determine how much 'fun' money each spouse will receive. Will the quantities be equal? Or is it proportionate to one's income? Expenses, perhaps? You will also need to determine which spending will come under the "fun" category. Will eating out as a couple, for example, be a shared expense or a pleasurable experience?

6.4 Create a Budget with Your Partner

In order to manage your household money, you must create a budget with your spouse. Your budget not only helps to plan and track where your money goes, but it also allows you to coordinate the direction of your finances.

You are not alone if you and your partner have never made a budget before. Only around 40% of Americans have a monthly family budget that closely analyses their spending, according to a survey.

Budgeting can be a delicate subject for couples, but it is possible to be effective and have fun while doing so. An important point to be mindful of when developing a budget with your spouse is that it is just a plan for your money, and like all plans, it should be debated, changed, and examined on a regular basis to ensure that you achieve your desired outcome.

Because there are so many different approaches to budgeting, it can be difficult to figure out how to do it. It all boils down to these basic steps:

- **Calculate Your Combined Income**

    It is critical to understand how much money you have to cover your costs and other budget things. Your income should, in fact, be the first line item on your budget.

    To begin, make a list of all of the anticipated income that you and your spouse will receive over the time period that you are budgeting for. It could be a week, two weeks, or even a month this time.

After you have made a list of all of your potential sources of income, figure out how much you intend to earn from each one. Add these figures up to get a total of how much money will be coming into the family to cover the budget's expenses. Make a note of this number at the top of your budget, and remember not to go over it.

- **Divide and Conquer**

  After you have calculated your total income, make a list of all of your anticipated expenses in one column. Some expenses are constant from month to month. For example, rent, electricity, and groceries are regular expenses that must be accounted for. These regular expenses can be divided into some categories for home budgeting.

  - Saving
  - Housing
  - Utilities
  - Transportation
  - Food
  - Medical
  - Personal Care

- Debt repayment
- Household goods
- Entertainment

Taking an average of what you have spent in the previous months is the simplest way to assess your spending. For example, take a three-month average of your grocery spending to create an estimate for the coming month. Sometimes, you will be able to determine the exact amount from a billing statement, while in others, you will just need to decide on a limit. This is true for a variety of expenses, including gifts and savings. Add up all of your estimations and remove them from your projected earnings. Is that more than your expected earnings? Then you will need to cut back on some of your spending. If it is less than your planned income, put the extra money toward savings or debt repayment.

- **Track Expenses**

The most crucial aspect of budgeting is keeping track of your expenses. After all, you need to know if you are on track to meet your financial goals.

6.5 Tackle Bills Effectively

There are two methods to go about this.

The first way is that every expense is divided in half. You each contribute the same amount to all bills, which will be used for any agreed-upon shared expenses such as housing, utilities, vacations, date evenings, and so on. You have complete control over your finances, yet you can easily split spending with your partner. The second way is that a portion of each person's paycheck is set aside for shared expenses. The individual who makes more money pays a higher percentage of the bills; the one who makes less money pays a lower percentage of the bills. You will pay 65 percent of the shared bills if you generate 65 percent of the revenue. You need to keep all of your accounts separate and then open a joint account in both of your names, ensuring that you have equal access to everything. Calculate each person's income proportion by finding out how much you and your partner make. Add up the total cost of all of your joint bills, then divide by your respective income percentages. This is the total amount that each individual must contribute.

Choose whether you wish to contribute to the shared account once a week, twice a week, or once a month.

The above-mentioned strategies are very important and valuable. Make sure that you keep them in mind while talking money with your partner.

Chapter 7: Say Yes to Appreciation

Appreciation is defined as the awareness and enjoyment of someone or something's positive features. We have all heard that appreciation has a significant impact on our personal happiness. This also pertains to our marital happiness. In a 2015 study, Barton and his colleagues discovered that expressing thankfulness for your spouse was strongly associated with marital satisfaction. When you take the time to appreciate the positive aspects of something or someone, they will feel cherished.

According to psychologists, a magic ratio of positive vs. negative encounters indicates the marriage's health. 5 to 1 is the magic ratio. To balance out each unfavorable encounter, at least 5 positive interactions are required. Our brains are programmed to dwell on the negative. News and interactions that are unfavorable stick with us significantly longer than positive ones. If a couple is always fighting and the conflict is full of negative exchanges, this is not a healthy relationship.

As a couple progresses through life together, every marriage has its ups and downs. Be mindful that you lift each other in the difficult times. It is a pleasant interaction every time you praise your spouse for something and let them know how much you appreciate them.

It shows them that you respect, love, and care about them and that you do not take them for granted.

There are three levels when it comes to expressing your appreciation to your spouse. They are:

- **Appreciating Who They Are**

  When we say, "I know who you are and I see you. You have value because you are you," this kind of gratitude touches the very heart of their being. It is when you consider their personality and character, reinforcing your admiration for them as a person. What characteristics do you notice in your spouse? On what qualities would they like your encouragement? For instance,

  - "I admire how you think. I love how wise you are."

  - "I admire your self-control. You motivate me."

  - "I admire your kindness. You are so concerned for other's pain."

  - "I respect your bravery. You do not back down from a challenge."

- **Appreciating What They Do**

    This clearly indicates that we are simply observing our spouse's efforts to improve our home and marriage. We value the positive aspects of their presence in our lives.

    We should express gratitude in our home for the everyday activities that are so easily taken for granted.

    > "I appreciate that you always have clean clothes for me."
    > "Thank you for the food."
    > "Our yard looks so good. Thank you for cutting the grass today."
    > "It is great that you fill up my car so I do not have to."

    It is easy to dismiss this as being too insignificant to discuss. After all, are not these things just part of the deal in a marriage? No, nothing should be expected, and everything should be appreciated. You can never thank your spouse enough for everything they do.

- **Appreciating How They Sacrifice**

    There are some sacrifices that your spouse makes for the two of you. Maybe you do not think of them as a sacrifice, but your partner does. Alternatively, you may perceive what they do as a sacrifice, and they do not make it. Acts of sacrifice should be greeted with gratitude and acknowledgment in any case. This fills your spouse's sails with wind and pushes them forward.

    Where do you see your partner sacrificing for you or your family, for example? Perhaps they have decided to avoid purchasing something they want in order to provide for the children. Perhaps they forego sleep in order to improve the family's work schedule. You could see someone going out of their way to help you or others with errands. Recognize sacrifice whenever you see it, and tell your spouse how much you appreciate what they have done.

Let's study these levels in detail. You can adopt the followings ways when showing appreciation and gratitude to your partner.

7.1 Show Vocal Gratitude

Couples seek counseling for a lot of reasons, including communication challenges, marital imbalance, financial issues, and parenting style differences. What I have observed, and what many other therapists have seen, is that laundry, dishwashing, and grocery difficulties are rarely about the laundry, dishes, or groceries. "You did the laundry wrong" might sometimes be code for something much complicated. It is usually a sign that there is an unmet demand in the relationship.

Using two words, "thank you," can improve a couple's bond, intimacy, and closeness.

According to new research, expressing gratitude to your partner may be the single most effective method to keep your marriage healthy. Some studies claim that saying "please" and "thank you" is just as crucial as sex. According to University of Georgia experts, saying "thank you" and showing gratitude might operate as an efficient divorce barrier and affect how committed partners feel in their relationship. Gratitude can help mitigate the harmful effects of conflict and bad encounters, according to the researchers.

- **Better Communicators**

    Saying "thank you" forces us to consider what we are actually grateful for, as well as how we communicate our gratitude to our relationships. Thanking your partner for going grocery shopping, for example, may appear insignificant, but it might express gratitude for a variety of other things beneath and beyond the grocery shopping. In other words, we can recognize our partners' desire to invest in the growth of a shared relationship when we are able to reflect on the meaning of their efforts. It is rarely about the groceries, as it is with the laundry. In this situation, the groceries have the potential to signify a deeper bond and a shared desire to help one another. We grow better at communicating and so connecting when we are able to truly perceive and appreciate our partners' efforts, especially when we are looking consciously and attentively.

- **Shifting Perspective**

    Rather than focusing on what we believe to be our partners' negative or less-than-perfect features, adopting a grateful posture and expressing gratitude with the words "thank you" turns our focus to our spouses' positive, appealing qualities. The phrase "thank you" can thus be used to express gratitude for our partners' gifts, efforts, and wishes. Just "thank you for all you do to make our house comfortable" might go a long way instead of fixating on what is not being done correctly.

- **Empowering Each other**

    As the cliché goes, cultivating an attitude of thankfulness may be empowering. It gets simpler to see what is possible as you develop the ability to see the gifts you have at your disposal, especially in your partnership.

- **Cultivating New Patterns**

    For many couples, breaking old communication patterns might be difficult. Practicing new ones can also help. Hearing the words "thank you" after one partner succeeds at changing can be a significant encouragement for further improvement.

    "Thank you for listening," say the next time your partner listens rather than reacting aggressively with you," I felt understood and heard, and I appreciate being able to express myself to you."

This "thank you" can be a strong encouragement for your partner to stick with the new routine. More importantly, you may both see the positive effects of the communication shift, which can help you trust that a new pattern will work and bring you closer together.

7.2 Understand the Power of Small Gestures

It is all too easy to get very comfortable once you think you are in a serious relationship that you forget to recognize your own spouse, the other half of this lovely duet. However, according to Hauser, a family therapist, it is critical to take time to acknowledge your partner in some way every day, even if it is just saying hello and goodbye when they walk in and out the door. She describes that one of the pillars of gratitude is recognizing that something or someone is truly important to you, and one of the best ways to accomplish so is through small actions like saying good morning and good night, kissing them hello and goodbye, and simply lingering to chat when they walk in the door. Those small gestures add up to the big thing: demonstrating to your partner that you actually care about their presence in your life. If you throw away those everyday moments, you may wind up sending a message to your spouse that they do not matter to you as much as you know deep down.

Pay attention to subtle gestures. They are more important than you believe since they help you show your partner that they are the most important person in your life. Here are a few tips for you:

- Bring home flowers to your partner to cheer them up. If you know what kind they like it would be the best.

- Bring them breakfast in bed after a rough day at work.

- Give them a helping hand whenever you have friends over or in basic everyday chores. Lighten their burden.

- Leave notes for them to encourage them and show your love and support.

- Surprise them by cooking their favorite meal.

- Send texts during the day to check up on them.

7.3 Publically Acknowledge Your Partner

Do you know that how you communicate to your family, friends, and even strangers about each other can foretell your relationship's success? According to a research study, starting six months into their marriages, 95 couples were monitored for ten years. The first hour of their one-on-one interview focused on their marriage, their parents' bond, and their own marriage philosophy.

Researchers also noted if couples exhibited liking and appreciation for their partner, completed each other's sentences, talked about each other as one unit, and found references around each other when telling stories. They found that couples who converse about each other in this way are considerably more likely to have a long-term relationship.

The researchers were even able to predict whether a couple would wind up divorced with 87 percent accuracy using only this information. The couples that had long-lasting marriages pictured their spouses in flattering terms, according to the survey. The ones who eventually divorced spoke cynically about their marriage. Consider that for a moment. The way you talk about your partner reveals a lot about the state of your relationship.

How is it possible? Actually, it boils down to the fact that your attitudes have an impact on how you perceive your spouse. If you openly compliment your spouse, you will invariably see him or her in a more favorable light and develop a stronger affection for him or her than you did previously. To put it another way, how you think, feel, and act is shaped by what you say about your partner, for better or worse. That is why maintaining strong public relations for your relationship is beneficial to both of you.

Nevertheless, apparently innocent complaints about marriage can easily creep into our social interactions. Even for people who have been married for years, it is a typical communication issue. Here are some pointers on acknowledgement that can help your marriage:

- **Make a 24-Hour Goal:** What would you highlight right now if you had to choose one item you admire about your partner? It is likely that you will need some time to think about it. We usually do not always notice and recall the qualities we love in our partners. So here is the task: Look for something to publicly compliment your partner on, and then tell someone about it the next day.

- **Compliment Your Partner from the Heart**: You can say things like, "Ann really knows how to keep our house organized; without her, we would be a mess." Or, "Adam is such a wonderful father; he constantly makes time to connect meaningfully with each of our children. "But forget it if you are giving compliments without actually meaning them.

- **Share Your Partner's Accomplishments:** The only people who enjoy blowing their own horn are narcissists. But it does not mean you have to remain silent about your spouse's accomplishments. Be the one to tell your family or friends any wonderful news about your partner. Say stuff like, "Stanley may not mention it, but his company received a large grant this week," or "Ann would not tell you, but she got a huge promotion at work."

7.4 Keep a Gratitude Journal

For some couples, this may sound a little woo-woo, but Hauser, a family therapist, claims that it has a very high success probability with her clientele. Here's how it works: You and your partner both keep a journal somewhere in the house that is easily accessible, such as your kitchen counter or your desk, and you both write down little notes of gratitude for each other every couple of days—anything from a "thank you for making the bed today" to meaningful song lyrics that you remember your partner knows by heart to simple words "I love you."

Hauser explains that because you are both taking the time to show each other that you care, the diary itself ends up being an act of gratitude. Plus, she adds, there are some things you can write to each other but not say to one other, particularly after a disagreement.

These are some of the ways you can show your admiration and gratitude to your partner every day, strengthening your love for each other.

Chapter 8: Say Yes to Forgiveness

When forgiveness is not a key principle in a marriage, it tends to become stuck. When issues develop, some couples fall into a tit-for-tat cycle in which brinkmanship and "settling the score" take precedence over dealing with and managing anger.

In order to have a happy marriage, you must be willing to forgive each other. To achieve marital fulfillment, your and your partner's ability to seek and grant forgiveness is critical. In marriage, forgiveness allows you to step out of the victim's position and demonstrate that you are capable of acknowledging and moving on from your suffering. In marriage, forgiveness is a skill that allows couples to resolve bad feelings and behaviors in order to strengthen their bond.

Forgiving a partner who has harmed you or made you furious can be the most difficult thing to do in a relationship. You must let go of your bitterness at your partner in order to let go of their wrongdoings.

Trying to punish your partner by repressing your unpleasant emotions and acting icily or distantly is extremely damaging to your relationship. Working over these feelings, on the other hand, is a big step that takes a lot of willpower to get past your partner's mistakes.

Here are some reasons why every marriage needs forgiveness:

- We affirm our trust, love, and acceptance of our spouse when we forgive them. We let them know that their blunder will not define our relationship. This is critical. We run the risk of accumulating up offenses that eventually destroy our relationship if we let our partner's mistakes determine the outcome of our marriage. It is critical to remember the context of this. Here, I am not talking about persistent bad behavior or neglect.

- Forgiveness ensures that you and your spouse keep short accounts. Allowing disappointments, hurts, and wounds to build up in a marriage is one of the most harmful things that can happen. One transgression follows another, and before you know it, you are facing a mountain to climb in order to reconnect and rebuild trust in your relationship. We keep the record clean and our list small when we practice forgiveness on a regular basis. When we are disappointed, this permits us to move on.

- We all know that when we hurt someone, we experience feelings of shame and guilt. We are remorseful for what we did to someone else. The road to redemption is eased with forgiveness. It is the doorway that allows our spouse to be free of guilt and shame.

- Forgiveness liberates us in two ways: first, it liberates the offender, and second, it liberates the victim. Forgiveness benefits and relieves the forgiver as much as the forgiven person, if not more. It frees us from the shackles of un-forgiveness, which eventually leads to resentment. And holding on to resentment does no one any good, especially you.

- Whether or whether not our partner has asked for forgiveness, there will be occasions when we must forgive them. Remember that you are releasing yourself from the prison of resentment while you do this, and graciously provide forgiveness to your partner.

Following are some guidelines to go through with this process:

8.1 Set Your Perspective

After experiencing injustice or betrayal, it is healthy and natural to need to process and handle challenging feelings. Staying with those feelings can be excruciatingly difficult, especially at first. Distance and thought can assist you in examining the situation objectively.

Does remembering the wrongdoing make you want to punish or harm the other person? Or are you willing to accept that a number of complex circumstances may have played a role in what you experienced?

If you realize that people in pain frequently cause their own pain, it can help you grow compassion without diminishing or condoning their wrong behavior.

It is also worth evaluating whether you are still in pain as a result of the betrayal or because your recollections of it are keeping you stuck in a downward spiral. If the latter is the source of your pain, making the choice to forgive can help you let go of those memories.

It takes a lot of effort on your side to forgive. You cannot just say, "I forgive you," and put it behind yourself if you wish your forgiveness to mean something.

It is possible that you might never understand why somebody did something. However, forgiving necessitates examining your pain and anger and deciding to let it go. This usually entails gaining a better knowledge of the other person and their situation. Without empathy and compassion, it is impossible to truly forgive.

Deciding on forgiveness is merely the first step; memories of your pain may reappear even after you have made the decision to forgive. Having patience and compassion on your side can help you succeed.

8.2 Look at the Bright Side

You are maybe not in a place to identify anything positive that resulted from the scenario when someone upsets you. You might have more emotional space in the future to realize what you have acquired.

Let's say your spouse has been unfaithful to you.

You were able to accept that the relationship was not working out after the initial betrayal. Of course, their infidelity was not the best decision, but it did reveal the relationship's flaws. Perhaps a close friend was harsh to you or abandoned you without explanation. In spite of your anguish and grief, you looked into why.

They eventually revealed that they were suffering from severe mental health problems, and you assisted them in finding care. Even if you cannot think of a specific benefit, embracing compassion and understanding may simply make you feel better. Here is something that might help you find the silver lining:

- Recognize and then let go of negative thoughts. Do not try to brush away bad thoughts about another person when you have them. You will only think about something more if you are actively trying not to think about it. Instead, acknowledge and then let go of how you are feeling.

    If you have a negative thought, give it a name. "Right now, I am angry at my wife," for example. Then, without focusing on the thought, let it pass. Keep in mind while you may not be able to control your thoughts, you are not obligated to participate with them.

- If you have a negative thought, put a positive thought in its place. It is natural to have resentments in life, and actively engaging with them by looking for a bright side can assist.

For example, if you think, "I'm upset at my husband as he did not remember our wedding anniversary." Now consider something along the lines of, "It is good to feel these emotions because they guide the two of us to work through our problems together."

- Practicing loving-kindness meditation is a good idea. Meditation on loving-kindness might help you feel more cheerful and forgiving of others. To begin, go somewhere quiet and sit in a position that is comfortable for you.

  Imagine people who adore you and care about you. Imagine them standing all around you, wishing you well. Then, send positive thoughts towards them. Imagine people in your life whom you wish them well. Think like this: "I wish you happiness. I wish you the best of luck."

  Then imagine a group of people that are completely neutral. These are people you do not know well, such as a coworker or a grocery store clerk. Consider them with comparable good sentiments.

  Finally, imagine someone who has wronged or harmed you. Even if you have bad feelings about them, send them positive thoughts.

- Accept what you cannot change and move on. The one thing you truly have the power to change is your own mindset at the end of the day. You cannot make people change. Do not consider forgiveness as a way to assist someone else in improving themselves. Consider it an opportunity to improve yourself by learning to be at peace and more sympathetic.

8.3 Make Room for Empathy

Scientists have researched what happens in the brain when we think about forgiveness and discovered that when people picture forgiving someone, their neural circuits linked to empathy exhibit higher activity. This indicates that empathy is related to forgiveness and is a crucial phase in the process.

When you look at some of the specifics in the life of the person who has wronged you, you can often see the wounds he carries more clearly and begin to feel empathy for him.

While you do not have to agree with what the other person did to you, putting yourself in the other person's position can help you forgive more easily. According to research, empathy has been linked to forgiveness, especially in men, and can make the process go more smoothly.

Rather than perceiving them as "the enemy," try to comprehend the issues they were facing. Were they experiencing a particularly trying period in their lives? Have you ever committed a mistake like this? You may find it easier to forgive if you recall the other person's positive traits and presume that their motives were not to intentionally harm you unless you have convincing evidence to the contrary.

8.4 Put Your Misery Behind Yourself

Express the pain you felt as a result of the hurt, whether to the other person or merely to get it out of your system like writing in a journal, venting to a friend, or writing a letter you never send to the other person. Get everything out of your system at once. This will also support you in determining the source of your discomfort.

Are you an active participant or a helpless victim in your own life? Will you let your suffering define you? Or are you someone more complex and deeper than that?

You have the option to continue to feel awful about another person's conduct or start to feel happy at any time for yourself. You must take charge of your own happiness rather than entrusting it to another individual. Why would you give someone who has wronged you in the past such influence in the present?

No amount of ruminating has ever solved a relationship problem. So, why do you choose to connect with and invest so much energy in these negative thoughts?

Stop reliving the misery of the past and let it go. Stop giving yourself that story in which the protagonist "you" is the victim of someone else's heinous deeds. You cannot change the past. All you can do is to make today your finest day ever.

When you concentrate on the now, you have less time to reflect on the past. When memories from the past resurface in your mind, take the time to notice them. After then, gently pull yourself back into the present now. Some people find it simpler to do this with a cognitive cue, such as telling themselves, "It is okay. That was in the past, and now I am concentrating on the present."

These are some of the key points that will help you heal and forgive your partner. Remember, it is okay to feel hurt and betrayed, but you have a choice to stay with the hurt or move on. Forgive your partner for him/her but most importantly, for yourself.

Chapter 9: What to Do and What Not to Do

Relationships can be difficult, and they almost always include some challenges. If you are lucky, you will pick up on the warning signs before they become too serious. There are some that are self-evident, such as emotional, verbal, or physical abuse, which are grounds for ending things. And a lot of drama, such as yelling, constant squabbling, crying, and emotional roller coasters, rarely suggests a happy marriage.

Then there are the blunders that are less visible. Those things, if neglected or unaddressed, will cause stress and may even jeopardize your happily ever after. Let's understand them so we can be wary of them.

9.1 The Don'ts of Marriage

Many long-term couples set themselves up for failure by engaging in the same negative practices over and over again. Some of these frequent relationship blunders, on the other hand, are absolutely avoidable. Do not worry if you have made one or more of the mistakes listed below. Every relationship entails some level of learning and development. Recognize areas where you can improve, and then get to it.

- **Pretending Everything is Okay**

    Some issues or insults may appear so blatant that you cannot imagine your partner failing to notice they have done anything wrong. So, rather than confronting the issue, you remain silent and moan about how they do not seem to care that you are upset. It is considerably easier and less terrible to respond "nothing" when asked, "What is wrong?" It is a Band-Aid solution for the time being, but the problem still exists. You can either stay angry and bitter or move on and brush the unsolved issue under the rug, only for it to resurface days, weeks, or months later with even more nastiness.

- **Bringing the Past into the Present**

    When attempting to settle current concerns, a couple may shift their focus to past ones. Maybe they still have a grudge or believe the new issue is the result of prior poor practices. In any case, doing so will render your arguments ineffectual and unconstructive, especially if the two of you have already agreed that the previous issues have been settled. Concentrate on the problem you are dealing with right now, figure out how to go forward, and do not bring up old arguments. This way, you can avoid fighting over the same issues in the future.

- **Make Arguments About Winning**

    Couples fight for a number of reasons; some fight to discover solutions, while others simply want to release their anger and frustrations on one other. Some go even further; they argue to prove that they are always correct, keeping score between themselves as to who was correct in the last dispute, who was the loser, and who won this time. Keep in mind that you and your partner are on the same team while you are married. As a result, his loss is also your loss and vice versa. Consider all of the bickering and disputing as an opportunity to reach an agreement and resolve any differences between you.

- **Not Talking Money Enough**

    Another common mistake made by most married couples is not being completely honest with one another about their financial condition or concerns. The wife may keep receipts from her extravagant shopping sprees hidden from her husband, or the husband may spend a large portion of his money in a business enterprise without informing his wife.

Given that financial issues are one of the leading causes of divorce, we cannot emphasize enough the need, to be honest with one another when it comes to household finances. A husband and wife should be aware of the amount of money they earn, spend, invest, owe, lend, or borrow. Keeping a loophole in this area will only lead to difficulty in the future. So, try to talk about your financial problems on a regular basis, and hopefully, you will be able to solve them or accomplish a common objective together.

- **Keeping Secrets**

    This is a factor that goes hand in hand with maintaining open lines of communication — do not keep secrets. You do not have to tell the other person everything about your life, but you should not conceal something important from them on purpose. When you feel even a little remorse for not telling them, you know it is a secret that needs to be shared. It will be released at some point, and sooner is always preferable to later.

- **Taking Your Partner for Granted**

  When we have been in a relationship for a long time, the novelty of the connection wears off. Things that used to come easy to us, like organizing enjoyable date evenings, surprise our partner with a gift, and giving them love praises, start to fade away.

  It is frequently the result of our focus shifting to other aspects of our lives, such as employment or financial commitments. We have no intention of making our partner feel unappreciated. We are simply overburdened with duties and oblivious to how our actions influence our partner, but still, that does not make it right. Your marriage needs to stay deserving of every effort.

- **Being Too Negative**

  Many of us naturally concentrate on the flaws in our relationship and what we would like to change about our spouse. While acknowledging the things that are not working in the relationship and taking efforts to address them can be beneficial, it can frequently distract us from what is working and the wonderful things that our partner does for us.

These were some key points to avoid that can help you keep your marriage away from falling apart. Is there anything more you should bear in mind for your marriage to be healthy and happy? Yes. Read ahead.

9.2 The Dos of Marriage

I wanted to end this book with some little tips for you that you should be mindful of in your marriage. Do not take the following points for granted because they are crucial to your success as a married couple:

- **Respect Each Other**

    One of the fastest tricks to kill a relationship is to have no respect for it or to lose respect for it. Couples fall apart for a number of reasons, one of which is a lack of respect. It has an impact on their love and intimacy, resulting in a difficult-to-recovery disconnection. The level of respect that spouses have for one another determines how happy they are in their marriage. Marriage depends heavily on marital respect. As a result, maintaining or reviving it is critical. In what aspects can you show your respect to your partner? Here you go:

➢ You lose sight of the worth of your connection when your relationship becomes more emotionally strained. You focus on the flaws and disappointments in your partner's behavior rather than attempting to correct them. Consider how you communicate with your partner, what you say, and how you say it. Respect can be re-established if both couples do so. Simply said, treat your partner the way you want to be treated. Reconnect with the love feelings of kindness, compassion, gratitude, and appreciation by remaining calm, sitting quietly, and opening up your heart for your spouse, listening to them.

➢ Your partner is entitled to their own thoughts and feelings. You should not belittle or injure your spouse because of a lack of agreement. When you first meet your mate, be compassionately curious. Look them in the eyes, retain an open heart, and think about the qualities you admire in your relationship. Remember that you and your partner are both doing the best you can and, for the most part, are in the same boat as you. Maintaining respect over the life of a relationship takes a lot of effort and patience. Treating your spouse with disrespect, indifference, and negativity encourages them to behave in the same way. Accept others' points of view, value their contributions, maintain the lines of communication open so you can make decisions together, and compromise when necessary.

- ➢ Do your part and make an effort to create a polite and loving environment, rather than calling your spouse out when you disagree with their behavior or instructing them how to act. Because you are leading by example, this strategy is effective.

- **Do Not Expect Your Partner to Complete You**

    Nowadays, the countless online dating sites encourage the overpowering sense that there are infinite options in the world, trapping some of us in a cycle of continual looking, or "relationshopping," as one study put it. We may unknowingly find ourselves looking for perfection or a single individual who can complete us, meet all of our needs and wants and make us whole. The truth is nobody can complete us.

To expect a partner to meet all of our emotional, bodily, and mental requirements is much beyond what they should be expected to do. To put it another way, expecting your partner to make you whole is completely illogical and unfair. I believe that being with someone you love may and will provide you happiness and support, but nobody can do your growth for you, no matter how much you wish for it. They can only assist you on your journey.

Instead of waiting for someone to come along and complete you, work on yourself. Determine what is missing in your life and why it is absent. Look for techniques to make you happy and satisfied.

And, if you are currently in a relationship, asking your spouse to support you as you grow and navigate yourself is far better for your relationship and more equitable.

- **Cultivating Patience**

Take a moment to rate your patience level on a scale of one to ten, with ten being "practically patient in every situation." Which one do you fall on the scale? On that scale, where would your partner rate you? If you are low on that scale, practice the following:

- When you feel like you are about to explode with rage, take a deep breath and let it go. Try to keep your wrath in check until you are calm and collected, and avoid using vulgar language. Consider the impact your angry comments will have on your partner.

- It is necessary that you listen to your spouse patiently in order to make them feel at ease while talking with you. Instead of making a snap choice, listen to what they have to say about the problem and then respond accordingly.

- Get away for a while and let the issue calm off to avoid needless confrontations with your spouse. Act with maturity and patience.

- When confronted with a challenging scenario, maintain your composure and tolerance for the situation. This will result in a viable solution to the issue.

- Take some time to yourself. Allow yourself and your spouse to spend some quality time together so that your stress levels are lower.

- Do not try to impose yourself on your partner all of the time. Allow them to work as they like, and if something bothers you, politely discuss it with them.

These were the three basic factors that should be a part of every marriage. Remember these dos and don'ts when you incorporate the seven secrets of a healthy and satisfying marital relationship.

Conclusion

Marriage has the potential to be one of the most wonderful experiences of your life. It can be tremendously satisfying to have a life partner with someone you can share your experiences, spend time with, and rely on in both good and bad times. Relationships can be beneficial to one's life satisfaction, well-being, and stress management, but they are not without their difficulties. These issues can put a couple's relationship under strain, but how they deal with them can either strengthen or weaken their bond, depending on how they handle the obstacles they experience.

Let's be real. Life's most beautiful events often appear to have some difficulties. We all know how difficult marriage can be. Is not there something inherently profound about two people making a commitment to each other? Simultaneously, there are countless accounts from married people regarding the difficulties of this commitment. What is it about a marital relationship that makes it so challenging? What are the most difficult aspects of being married?

This book caters to the major problematic areas of any marital relationship and how you can overcome them. There are seven secrets we talk about in the book to a healthy, happy, and fulfilling marriage.

The first chapter is focused on the bliss of marriage, i.e., what it can do for you both mentally and physically. This chapter will help you figure out why marriage is worth fighting for. A boost in emotional security, happiness, mental health, physical health, longevity, and financial status are of the many perks of marriage. Before we get into that, we discuss why marriage is so hard. Mental adjustment, preconditioned fantasy mindset, and communication are the top reasons.

The next seven chapters entail the seven rewarding secrets of a joyous marriage.

The second chapter is devoted to active communication. Here we briefly discuss the importance of effective communication between couples and then describe strategies in detail to achieve it, i.e., active listening, active speaking, and non-verbal communication.

The third chapter is associated with a fundamental pillar of marriage "understanding." Exploring yourself, learning your partner's love language, nurturing curiosity in yourself, practicing empathy, and honestly opening up your partner are key elements of developing an understanding of your partner.

The fourth chapter is about maintaining intimacy, and we discuss the importance of four kids of intimacy, i.e., emotional intimacy, recreational intimacy, physical intimacy, and intellectual intimacy. Making new moments together, learning to be vulnerable, showing physical affection, and accepting your partner while avoiding comparison are some of the strategies to develop an intimate relationship with your partner.

The fifth chapter explains the significance of making time for your partner. Evaluating quality time together, sharing a year calendar, putting the tech away and planning date night regularly are some of the effective ways you can spend time with your loved one.

The sixth chapter deals with managing finances. We discuss the factors that can contribute to financial issues and then eventually how we can rescue ourselves from hitting rock bottom. Talking it out with your partner, deciding on separate or combined finances, designating fun money, creating a budget with your partner, and tackling bills effectively are some of the ways you can keep yourself from a financial disaster.

The seventh chapter is about appreciation and gratitude. We discuss the three levels of appreciation and then go through the ways we can go about them, i.e., showing vocal gratitude, understanding the power of small gestures, publically acknowledging your partner, and keeping a gratitude journal.

The eighth chapter focuses on forgiveness. We point out why we need forgiveness in a marriage and then move on to the steps to help you forgive your partner, i.e., setting your perspective, looking at the bright side, making room for empathy, and putting your misery behind yourself.

The final chapter of the book briefly mentions the dos and don'ts of a healthy marriage. The don'ts include pretending everything is okay, bringing the past into the present, making arguments about winning, not talking money enough, keeping secrets, taking your partner for granted, and being too negative. The dos include respecting each other, not expecting your partner to complete you, and cultivating patience. The genuine thought behind writing this book is to help couples work on their marriage and enjoy a blissful relationship with each other. The chapters in this book are well researched and based on my personal and professional knowledge.

I hope this book guided you towards a better place in your marital relationship. If this book helps you improve your marital relationship in any way, leave a review on Amazon.